Understanding the
Articles of
Confederation

Sally Senzell Isaacs

Crabtree Publishing Company
www.crabtreebooks.com

Author: Sally Senzell Isaacs
Editor-in-Chief: Lionel Bender
Editor: Kelley MacAulay
Proofreaders: Adrianna Morganelli,
  Crystal Sikkens
Project editor: Robert Walker
Photo research: Susannah Jayes
Designer: Malcolm Smythe
Production coordinator: Katherine Kantor
Production: Kim Richardson
Prepress technician: Margaret Amy Salter
Consultant: Professor Richard Jensen,
  history teacher, consultant, and author

This book was produced for
  Crabtree Publishing Company
  by Bender Richardson White, U.K.

Cover:
  Colonial drummer at a U.S. Revolutionary War reenactment.
  Page one of the Articles of Confederation
Title page:
  George Washington enters New York City, soon to be made
  the first U.S. president
Photographs:
© Art Archive: Chateau de Blerancourt/Gianni Dagli Orti: p. 23
© iStockphoto.com: p. 27, 28 (bottom left), 29
© Library of Congress: p. 8 (cph 3g05315), 10 (cph 3b50118),
  13 (cph 3a18693—top right)
© Northwind Picture Archives: p. 4, 6 (left and right), 9, 11, 12,
  15, 16, 17, 19, 20, 21, 22, 24, 26
© Shutterstock.com: cover (right), p. 13 (bottom right)
© The Granger Collection: p. 1, 5, 7, 14, 18, 25
© US Department of Defense: p. 28 (bottom right)
© Wikipedia.com: cover (background)

Library and Archives Canada Cataloguing in Publication

Isaacs, Sally Senzell, 1950-
    Understanding the Articles of Confederation / Sally Senzell Isaacs.

(Documenting early America)
Includes index.
ISBN 978-0-7787-4372-9 (bound).--ISBN 978-0-7787-4377-4 (pbk.)

    1. United States. Articles of Confederation--Juvenile literature.
2. Constitutional history--United States--Juvenile literature. 3. United
States--Politics and government--1775-1783--Juvenile literature.
I. Title. II. Series: Isaacs, Sally Senzell, 1950- . Documenting early
America.

KF4508.I83 2008   j342.7302'9   C2008-905556-X

Library of Congress Cataloging-in-Publication Data

Isaacs, Sally Senzell, 1950-
    Understanding the Articles of Confederation / Sally Senzell Isaacs.
       p. cm. -- (Documenting early America)
    Includes index.
    ISBN-13: 978-0-7787-4377-4 (pbk. : alk. paper)
    ISBN-10: 0-7787-4377-2 (pbk. : alk. paper)
    ISBN-13: 978-0-7787-4372-9 (reinforced library binding : alk. paper)
    ISBN-10: 0-7787-4372-1 (reinforced library binding : alk. paper)

    1. United States. Articles of Confederation--Juvenile literature. 2.
Constitutional history--United States--Juvenile literature. 3. United
States--Politics and government--1775-1783. I. Title.

    KF4508.I823 2009
    342.7302'9--dc22

                                                2008036597

Crabtree Publishing Company

www.crabtreebooks.com   1-800-387-7650

Published in Canada
Crabtree Publishing
616 Welland Ave.
St. Catharines, Ontario
L2M 5V6

Published in the United States
Crabtree Publishing
PMB16A
350 Fifth Ave., Suite 3308
New York, NY 10118

Published in the United Kingdom
Crabtree Publishing
White Cross Mills
High Town, Lancaster
LA1 4XS

Published in Australia
Crabtree Publishing
386 Mt. Alexander Rd.
Ascot Vale (Melbourne)
VIC 3032

Contents

The First Steps 4

The British Colonies 6

Joining Together 8

Independence 10

A New Nation 12

Uniting the States 14

Joined in Friendship 16

Big and Small States 18

Maryland Says "No" 20

More Problems 22

A New Constitution 24

Big Changes 26

A Plan for the Future 28

Timeline 30

Websites, Further Reading 31

Glossary, Index 32

The First Steps

The year 1776 was an important one for the United States. This is the year that the nation was created! Before 1776, America was 13 separate **colonies** that belonged to Britain. A colony is a place where people live that is far from the country that rules it. People who live in a colony are called colonists.

▼ *This map shows the United States as it was in 1776.*

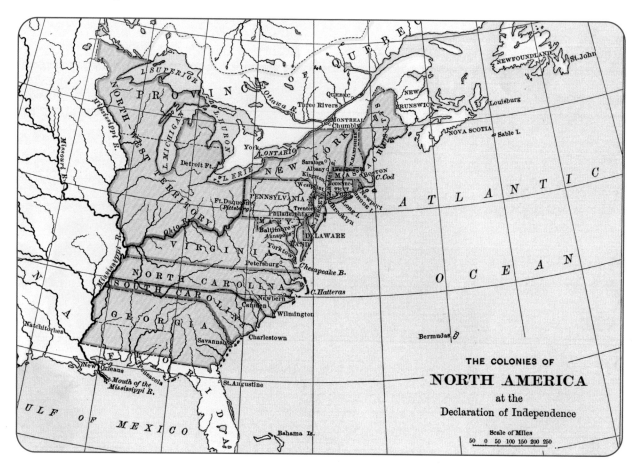

THE COLONIES OF
NORTH AMERICA
at the
Declaration of Independence

Writing out the plan

On July 4, 1776, the leaders of the colonies broke their ties with Britain. They decided to form a new country called the United States of America. The colonists became known as "Americans." The leaders of the colonies gathered together and wrote the **Articles** of **Confederation.** The Articles described how the leaders would run the country.

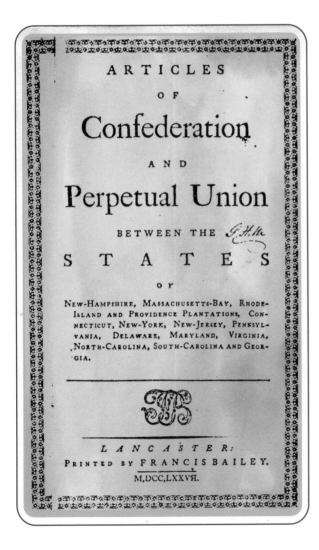

The Articles were not a perfect set of rules. In fact, after seven years, the leaders decided to start over and write a new set of rules. Although the Articles of Confederation were not used for very long, they were an important first step for the new country.

◄ *The Articles of Confederation are five pages long. The ink has faded over time.*

The British Colonies

Britain is a country in Europe, which is on the other side of the Atlantic Ocean from America. People from Europe founded the American colonies around 1600. Starting in the 1760s, Britain's King George III wanted to rule the colonies. Colonists had to follow Britain's laws and pay **taxes** to Britain. A tax is money that people pay to their **government** to run the country.

▲ *In 1765, colonists had to pay for a stamp like this one whenever they bought goods, such as cloth.*

▲ *Britain's King George III.*

The colonists take action

The colonists enjoyed being part of Britain for many years. Then King George III wanted the colonists to pay for the king's army and officials that lived in America. He demanded that the colonists pay new taxes. Items such as newspapers, sugar, tea, and cloth would now cost more.

The colonists grew angry about the new taxes. In 1773, some Massachusetts colonists climbed onto a British ship in the Boston Harbor. Disguised as Native Americans, they threw many chests of tea in the water. The tea was ruined. This act became known as the Boston Tea Party.

▶ *In protest of the tea tax, a group of colonists threw chests of tea into the Boston Harbor.*

Joining Together

After the Boston Tea Party, King George III closed the Boston Harbor. No food or other goods could reach Boston. The king sent more British soldiers to Boston. He told the colonists that they must allow the soldiers to stay in their homes. The colonists felt the king was very unfair.

In 1774, the colonial leaders called a meeting in Philadelphia, Pennsylvania. Each colony sent several **representatives** to speak for its people. The group of representatives was called the **Continental Congress**. It wrote letters to the king hoping he would change his ways and treat the colonists fairly.

JOIN, or DIE.

◀ *Benjamin Franklin, a colonist from Pennsylvania, made this cartoon. Each part of the snake represents a colony. If they joined together, the colonies would be like a powerful snake. If they did not join together, they would fail.*

8

War begins

In April 1775, British soldiers went to Lexington, Massachusetts. Colonial soldiers told the British to go home. A battle soon broke out between the two groups. It was the start of a six-year war. The war was called the **American Revolution**. A **revolution** is a strong move by people to change their government. Congress formed an army. They chose George Washington to lead the army.

▶ *George Washington was the general of the American army.*

Independence

While soldiers fought in the war, Congress discussed gaining **independence** from Britain. Many colonists did not want to be controlled by the king any longer. They wanted their own government. This government would have representatives to speak for the people. The representatives would make laws. Congress chose Thomas Jefferson, from Virginia, to write a Declaration of Independence. A **declaration** is a written or spoken announcement. In the Declaration, Jefferson announced that the colonies were free and independent states.

▶ *Thomas Jefferson and four other representatives who helped write the Declaration, presented it to Congress.*

A new government

In the Declaration of Independence, Jefferson wrote that *"all men are equal."* They all have the rights to *"life, liberty, and the pursuit of happiness."* King George III had been unfair to the colonists, and they would not stand for it any longer. This was a big step! On July 4, 1776, Congress voted "yes" to accept the Declaration and gain independence from Britain. The representatives celebrated. Then they got to work, starting a new government.

▼ *Colonists gathered in every town to hear the words of the Declaration of Independence.*

A New Nation

In the Declaration of Independence, Jefferson announced that the British colonies would become 13 states. Each state formed its own government. People elected representatives to make laws for their states. Each state had a **constitution**, or written plan for the government. A constitution says what the government can and cannot do.

▲ *States had their own lawmakers and governments.*

Writing a draft

John Dickinson led the committee to write the Articles of Confederation. He used many ideas that Benjamin Franklin had already written. On July 12, Dickinson read his draft of the Articles to Congress. Everyone made suggestions to improve it.

▶ *A portrait of John Dickinson*

Writing the plan

The states also wanted to join together as a nation. They needed to raise money for the new nation and plan a national government. They had to fight a war with Britain. Together, the states would fight common enemies and protect their freedom. They would help each other against all attacks, no matter what the reason. The plan was called the Articles of Confederation. A confederation is a group that works together.

▲ *An early American flag representing 13 states*

Uniting the States

When uniting the states, there were some important questions to answer. What powers would the states give up to the national government? Americans remembered Britain's unfair rules. They wanted the national government only to unite the states, not rule them. The governments of each state were to be stronger than the national government.

▼ *These ships are arriving in Boston with goods from Europe and southern states in about 1775. During the American Revolution, the British closed these ports.*

Settling their differences

When the national government was formed, the states became a nation called the United States of America. Were the states really united, however? In the southern states, most people raised crops on farms. Many owned **slaves**, who worked in the fields for no pay. In the northern states, many people depended on shipping to send and receive goods. The Articles of Confederation had to unite people who lived very differently from one another. The state leaders still had to be able to make laws that were good for the people of their states.

Slavery

For many years, slavery was allowed in all the states. After 1776, however, northern states started passing laws to end slavery in their states.

◄ *Many slaves worked on cotton plantations in the southern states.*

Joined in Friendship

After writing the Articles of Confederation, state leaders called the states a "league of friendship." The states kept most of their old power but the national government made laws for the entire nation. The new government would have a Congress made of representatives, called **delegates**, from each state. Congress would make decisions for the country. The country did not yet have a president.

Congress could declare war and control the army. It could ask the states for money to fight a war. The states did not have to give money to Congress, however. Congress could not make people pay taxes.

◀ *American soldiers*

Native Americans

Long before the colonists came to America, Native Americans lived throughout the land. As Europeans arrived, they took land away from Native Americans. The Articles of Confederation gave Congress the power to make **treaties**, or peace agreements, with Native Americans. However, most treaties forced Native Americans off their land.

▲ *Before 1776, most Native Americans lived peaceably in villages far from the colonists.*

Big and Small States

Each state had delegates in Congress. The delegates would vote on decisions. Some states were much bigger and had more people than did other states, however. The big states wanted more votes since the delegates represented more people. Small states did not think this was fair. If this happened, a smaller state would always be overpowered by a bigger state. The delegates argued about voting. Finally, they agreed; each state would get one vote.

▼ *Delegates rode horses to the meetings of Congress in Philadelphia.*

Spreading the word

Congress had many decisions to make about the American Revolution. Due to this, it took the delegates over a year to finish the Articles of Confederation. In November 1777, they finally agreed to everything in the document. A local printer made 300 copies. The delegates took the copies home to their states. The Articles were printed in newspapers everywhere. Next, the government of each state had to approve the Articles. This would take almost four more years.

▼ *A printing press was used to make copies of the Articles.*

▶ *Americans read about the Articles of Confederation in newspapers.*

Maryland Says "No"

The United States government would not be an official government until all the states had approved the Articles of Confederation. By 1779, every state except Maryland had approved the Articles. The Maryland delegates were worried that the bigger states were growing too strong.

In the late 1770s, there was still a lot of land to the west of the states that did not belong to any state. **Settlers** had started to move into this open land. States such as Virginia and New York claimed all the land to the west of them. Maryland's delegates would not accept the Articles until the big states gave that land to the national government.

◄ *Settlers lived in cabins.*

Agreement at last

Finally, the large states agreed to give up their land claims *"for the sake of the public good."* Congress added a new section to the Articles. It said that, as settlers moved to open land, new states would be formed. On March 1, 1781, Maryland accepted the Articles of Confederation, which became the first official government plan for the United States.

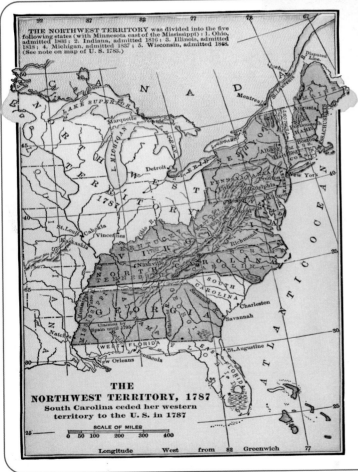

Spreading west

By 1787, the 13 states had expanded west and the land around the Great Lakes was set up as the Northwest Territory. Over time, it became the states of Ohio, Indiana, Illinois, Michigan, Wisconsin, and Minnesota.

◄ *This map shows the land in North America that was claimed by the United States in 1787.*

More Problems

The nation's first government had many problems. First, the states acted like 13 separate countries. Each state collected taxes but did not give enough money to Congress. Some states began to tax one another for goods that came across their borders. Second, during the American Revolution, soldiers needed uniforms, guns, food, and pay. Congress asked the states for money to pay for the army. Sometimes, the states refused to provide this money. Congress had to borrow money from other countries to pay for the war.

▼ *The states printed their own money. Some states would not accept money from other states, however.*

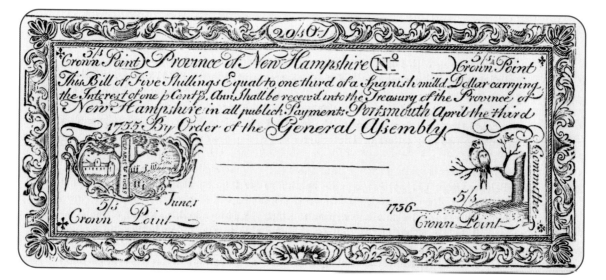

▲ *The American Revolution was fought at sea as well as on land. The states had to pay for fighting ships and sailors, too.*

A nation without a leader

Problems with the Articles of Confederation caused bad feelings within the national government. When the war was over in 1781, Congress could not pay back the money it had borrowed. The United States was quickly losing respect from other countries. At this time the national government had no leader, such as a president or king. There were no courts or judges in the government either. The country seemed weak because it had no leadership.

A New Constitution

In 1787, Alexander Hamilton said *"The nation is sick and wants powerful remedies (medicine)."* Hamilton was one of 55 delegates who attended a meeting in Philadelphia in May 1787. All the states except Rhode Island had sent delegates to the meeting. They met to fix the problems with the Articles. Before long, the delegates made a big decision. They decided the Articles of Confederation could not be fixed! The nation needed a new constitution and a president. Alexander Hamilton, George Washington, and James Madison were among those who wanted a stronger national government.

◄ *The delegates of the Constitutional **Convention** met at the Pennsylvania State House in Philadelphia. The Declaration of Independence had been signed here in 1776.*

A new way forward

The delegates chose George Washington to be the head of this meeting, which was called the Constitutional Convention. At the meeting, the delegates began writing a new constitution. They still wanted the new national government to share powers with the state governments, but the national government would be stronger than before. It would have the power to collect taxes and would control trading among the states and with other countries.

▼ *In April 1789, George Washington entered New York City, the nation's first capital, to become president under the new Constitution.*

Big Changes

The delegates did not want any one person or group in the United States to have too much power. So they made three **branches**, or sections, of government. Each branch had its own jobs. The legislative branch is called Congress. It makes the laws. The executive branch, led by the president, ensures that the laws are carried out. The president also leads the armed forces and makes agreements with other countries on behalf of the nation.

▲ *The first U.S. Congress met in this building in New York City.*

The third branch of government is the judicial branch. It is made up of the courts, which interpret, or explain, the laws. The courts make sure the president and Congress do not overstep their powers.

Keeping things in check

The United States government today is still made up of the three branches. The delegates created **checks and balances** for the three branches. For example, Congress can pass a law, but the president can veto, or stop, the law from going into effect. Federal judges can also change a law if they feel it goes against the Constitution.

▼ *The Capitol building in Washington D.C. is where Congress meets to make the nation's laws today.*

A Plan for the Future

The Constitution divides the Congress into two groups. One group is called the House of Representatives. States that have a lot of people send more representatives to the House of Representatives than do states that have fewer people. The other group of Congress is called the Senate. Each state sends two **senators** to the Senate. Both the Senate and the House of Representatives write laws.

▼ *The Internal Revenue Service building in Washington D.C., where taxes are now collected.*

▲ *Today, the U.S. government continues to pay for armed forces to protect the nation.*

Fit for all time

The delegates finished writing the Constitution in September 1787. In June 1788, nine states accepted it. That was enough to make it official. Four other states accepted the Constitution soon afterward. The United States had a new plan of government. The Constitution took the place of the Articles of Confederation.

The Articles of Confederation will always be remembered as the nation's first step toward unity. With the Articles, the states joined together. They sent representatives to make laws in a peaceful and orderly way. After 220 years, the United States government still runs this way today.

▶ *Americans still follow the guidelines set out in the United States Constitution.*

Timeline

1765 Britain passes the Stamp Act, which says colonists must pay taxes on newspapers and legal papers

1773 Angry about a tea tax, colonists dump tea in the Boston Harbor

1774 The Continental Congress meets in Philadelphia

1775 First shots of the American Revolution are fired in Lexington and Concord, Massachusetts

1776 The Continental Congress agrees to the Declaration of Independence; John Dickinson and his committee write the Articles of Confederation

1777 Congress agrees to the wording of the Articles

1781 The 13 states accept the Articles of Confederation; Britain loses the war; the first official government plan for the United States begins

1783 A peace treaty ends the American Revolution

1787 The Constitutional Convention begins; the U.S. Constitution is signed and sent to the states

1788 Nine states accept the Constitution, and it replaces the Articles of Confederation

1790 All 13 states approve the Constitution

Websites

1. Ben's Guide to U.S. Government for Kids
http://bensguide.gpo.gov/3-5/documents/articles/index.html
This site shows the original, handwritten Articles and includes links
to related subject areas.

2. The U.S. Constitution Online
http://www.usconstitution.net/articles.html#Preamble
Here you will find the complete text of the Articles and a list of all the signers.
The site also provides links to other Websites relating to the Constitution.

3. Congress for Kids
http://www.congressforkids.net/Independence_articles.htm
Here you will find the history of the Articles, plus a multiple-choice quiz and links
to other fun quizzes about the Articles and the Constitution.

4. Social Studies for Kids
http://www.socialstudiesforkids.com/articles/ushistory/articlesofconfederation1.htm
Visit this site for a full explanation of the Articles, along with a glossary, a clickable
map of the 13 colonies, and links to other related topics.

5. National Archives and Records Administration
http://www.archives.gov/exhibits/charters/declaration.html
This site includes a transcript of the Declaration, an image of the original
document, and links to other Websites of interest.

Further Reading

Callahan, Kerry P. *The Articles of Confederation.* New York: Rosen, 2003.

Feinberg, Barbara. *The Articles of Confederation.* Brookfield, CT: Twenty-first Century
Books, 2002.

Hossell, Karen Price. *The Articles of Confederation.* Chicago: Heinemann, 2004.

Isaacs, Sally Senzell. *America in the Time of George Washington.* Chicago: Heinemann, 1999.

Rebman, Renée C. *The Articles of Confederation.* Mankato, Minn.: Compass Point, 2006.

Rosen, Daniel. *Independence Now: The American Revolution 1763–1783.* Washington,
D.C.: National Geographic, 2004.

Swain, Gwenyth. *Declaring Freedom: A Look at the Declaration of Independence, the Bill
of Rights, and the Constitution.* Minneapolis: Lerner, 2004.

Glossary

American Revolution
The war of independence
from Britain

articles A set of rules

branch A part of a
large organization

checks and balances
Ways to stop one person
or group from having
too much power

colony A place where
people live far from the
country that rules it

confederation A group
that works together

constitution A written
plan for a government

Continental Congress A
group of representatives who
make laws and discuss issues

convention
An official meeting

declaration A written
or spoken announcement
to many people

delegate A person who
speaks or acts for other
people; a representative

government A group of
people who run a country

independence Being free
to do what one wants

representative Someone
who speaks for others when
laws are made

revolution A strong
move by people to
change their government

senators State
representatives
in the Senate

settlers People who move
to a new place to live

slave A person who is
owned by another person
and usually must work
for no pay

tax Money that
goes to run a country

treaty A written
agreement between
two groups or countries

Index

American Revolution 9, 14,
   19, 22, 23, 30
Articles of Confederation 5,
   13, 15, 16, 17, 19, 20, 21,
   23, 24, 29, 30
Britain 4, 5, 6, 7, 10, 11, 13,
   14, 30
colonies 4, 5, 6, 8, 10, 12
colonists 4, 5, 6, 7, 8, 10,
   11, 17, 30
Congress 8, 9, 10, 11, 13,
   16, 17, 18, 19, 21, 22, 23,
   26, 27, 28, 30
Constitution 12, 24, 25, 27,
   28, 29, 30
Declaration of Independence
   10, 11, 12, 24, 30
delegates 16, 18, 19, 20, 24,
   25, 26, 27, 29
Franklin, Benjamin 8, 13
Jefferson, Thomas 10,
   11, 12
King George III 6, 7, 8,
   10, 11
laws 6, 10, 12, 15, 16, 26,
   27, 28, 29
Native Americans 7, 17
president 16, 23, 24, 25,
   26, 27
representatives 8, 10,
   11, 12, 16, 28, 29
slaves 15
taxes 6, 7, 16, 22,
   25, 28
United States 4, 5, 15,
   20, 21, 23, 26, 27,
   28, 29, 30
Washington, George 9,
   24, 25

32

Printed in the U.S.A. – BG